MI'KMAQ

ABORIGINAL PEOPLES OF CANADA

Christine Webster

Published by Weigl Educational Publishers Limited
6325 10 Street S.E.
Calgary, Alberta, Canada
T2H 2Z9

Website: www.weigl.com

Library and Archives Canada Cataloguing in Publication

Webster, Christine
        Mikmaq : Aboriginal peoples of Canada / Christine Webster.
(Aboriginal peoples of Canada)
Includes index.
ISBN 978-1-55388-508-5 (bound).--ISBN 978-1-55388-515-3 (pbk.)
        1. Micmac Indians--Juvenile literature. I. Title.
II. Series: Aboriginal peoples of Canada (Calgary, Alta.)
E99.M6W433 2009   j971.004'97343   C2009-903520-0

Printed in the United States of America
1 2 3 4 5 6 7 8 9 0 13 12 11 10 09

Photograph and Text Credits
Cover: Canadian Museum of Civilization (III-F-79, a, b, D2004-22076); Alamy: pages 6, 12T, 21; Canadian Museum of Civilization: pages 1 (III-F-79, a, b, D2004-22076), 9M (III-F-259, D20040-24064), 12B (III-F-151, D2004-22800), 15B (III-F-183 a, b, D2004-22719), 17B (III-f-213 a, b, D2004-22836), 20 (III-F-79, a, b, D2004-22076), 23 (B-D-310, D2004-27600); Corbis: page 9B; CP Images: pages 4, 8, 16, 17T; Dreamstime: page 22; Getty Images: pages 5, 10L, 10M, 10R, 11L, 11M, 11R, 13T; 15T; Library and Archives Canada: page 7 (C-103533); McCord Museum: page 9T, 13B, 14.

We gratefully acknowledge the financial support of the Government of Canada through the Book Publishing Industry Development Program (BPIDP) for our publishing activities.

PROJECT COORDINATOR Heather Kissock
DESIGN Terry Paulhus, Kenzie Browne
ILLUSTRATOR Martha Jablonski-Jones

Contents

The People

The Mi'kmaq are a **First Nation** that live throughout eastern Canada. The term "Mi'kmaq" comes from the word *nikmak*. This means "my friends." Mi'kmaq is prounounced "meeg maw."

The Mi'kmaq have lived in eastern Canada for more than 10,000 years. In the past, the Mi'kmaq were hunter–gatherers. This means that their food came from hunting animals and gathering items found in nature.

NET LINK

"Mi'kmaq" is only one way to spell the name of this First Nation. To see other spellings, go to **http://museum.gov.ns.ca/mikmaq/?section=spelling**.

Mi'kmaq Homes

WIGWAMS

In the past, the Mi'kmaq lived in homes called wigwams. A wigwam was shaped like a cone or dome. Its frame was built using poles made out of spruce. The frame was covered with bark.

Mi'kmaq Ideas

The Mi'kmaq used birchbark to cover their wigwams because it does not let in water. Mi'kmaq families could stay inside their homes and not get wet when it rained or snowed.

Wigwams were designed to be built quickly and moved easily. A wigwam took about one day to build and was easily taken apart. The materials could be moved to different locations and used again.

Mi'kmaq Clothing

ROBES

In cold weather, Mi'kmaq men and women covered themselves with robes made from animal hides and furs. Men wore their robes like a blanket over their shoulders. Women wrapped their robes around their body under their arms. They tied them at the waist with a belt.

LEGGINGS

Both men and women wore leggings. The leggings were made from caribou or moose skins that were tied at the hip with a belt.

HEADDRESSES

Both men and women wore beaded headbands with feathers. Sometimes, women wore a pointed hat instead of a headdress.

BREECHCLOTHS

Mi'kmaq men wore animal-hide breechcloths that hung from their waist.

MOCCASINS

Both men and women wore moccasins on their feet. These shoes were made from animal skins and were decorated with quills or beads.

Hunting and Gathering

SEALS

In January, the Mi'kmaq hunted seals along the coast.

CARIBOU

From February to March, they hunted caribou and other game. The meat was dried and smoked to **preserve** it.

HERRING

In April, the Mi'kmaq returned to the coast to catch herring. Like game, the fish were dried and smoked.

The Mi'kmaq obtained their food mostly from the forests and the sea. They planned their lives around the **migration** cycles of the animals. Every few months, they moved to places where they knew certain animals would be found.

SHELLFISH Over the summer, the Mi'kmaq continued to fish. They also gathered shellfish, such as lobster.

BERRIES The summer was also a time to gather berries, roots, and other plants to eat.

COD In December, when the waters were frozen, the Mi'kmaq went ice fishing to catch cod.

Mi'kmaq Tools

BONES AND WOOD

The Mi'kmaq needed tools to cut wood and hunt animals. To make tools, the Mi'kmaq used many items from the natural world. Bones and wood were used to make sewing needles and other tools.

Mi'kmaq Ideas

The Mi'kmaq made a birchbark horn to help them hunt moose. When they blew into the horn, a sound similar to a moose call came out. This brought the moose to the Mi'kmaq hunters.

STONE

Knife blades were made by chipping at stones to give them sharp edges. The stone was then tied to a wooden stick to make an axe.

Moving from Place to Place

CANOES

The Mi'kmaq lived near oceans, lakes, and rivers. Water travel was a very important part of their lives. To travel by water, they relied on birchbark canoes. Mi'kmaq canoes had wide bottoms with raised ends. Their sides curved upward in the middle. This shape allowed the Mi'kmaq to use their canoes at sea, as well as in streams.

Mi'kmaq Ideas

Being able to stay on top of deep snow helped the Mi'kmaq when hunting. Heavy animals would sink into the snow. They could not run as fast as the hunters.

SNOWSHOES

In the summer, the Mi'kmaq travelled the land by foot. In the winter, they used snowshoes. The wide paddle of the snowshoes helped the Mi'kmaq walk on top of deep snow without sinking. Snowshoes are still used by the Mi'kmaq today.

Mi'kmaq Music and Dance

Dancing is a way for the Mi'kmaq to tell stories and entertain others. Sometimes, dancers tell the story of a successful hunt. The dancer pretends to be the hunter or the animal.

NET LINK

Learn to sing a Mi'kmaq song at
www.firstnationhelp.com/ali/mikmaw-song.php.

As in the past, singing and drumming are an important part of Mi'kmaq **spirituality**. The Mi'kmaq use drums in ceremonies, and for dancing and singing. The drum represents the centre of life.

How Rabbit Received His Long Ears

When Rabbit was first put on Earth, he had short ears. One day, he was bored and decided to play a trick on the other animals. He told Beaver that the Sun was not going to rise again.

Beaver became worried and told the other animals. These other animals told their friends, and, soon, the whole animal world was in a panic. They all began to prepare for the loss of the Sun.

Glooscap, a caring Mi'kmaq spirit, saw the animals behaving strangely. He asked them what was happening. When they told him what they had heard, he knew it was not true. He then asked who had said this to them.

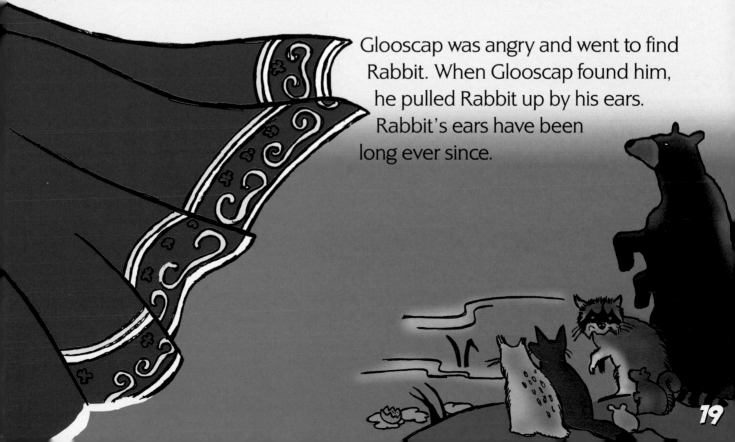

Glooscap was angry and went to find Rabbit. When Glooscap found him, he pulled Rabbit up by his ears. Rabbit's ears have been long ever since.

19

Mi'kmaq Art

The Mi'kmaq were well known for their porcupine quillwork. Each quill was dipped into brightly coloured paints. The coloured quills were used to create designs on items, such as chairs and boxes.

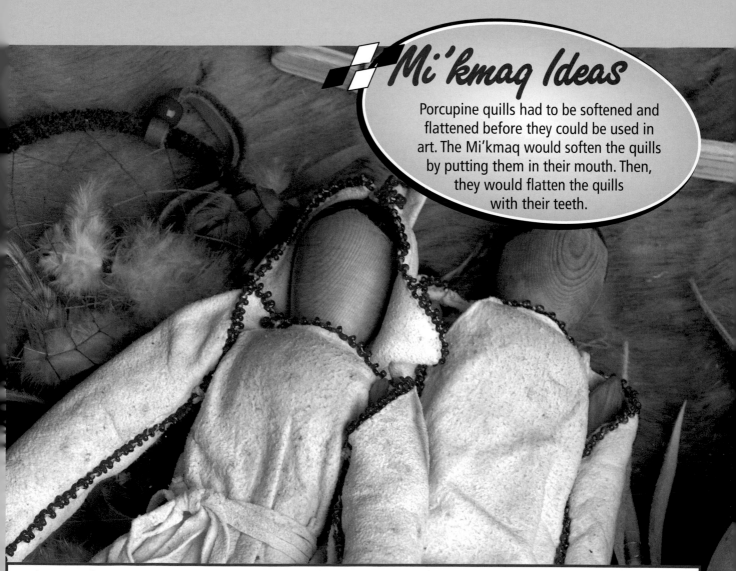

Mi'kmaq Ideas

Porcupine quills had to be softened and flattened before they could be used in art. The Mi'kmaq would soften the quills by putting them in their mouth. Then, they would flatten the quills with their teeth.

The Mi'kmaq were also known for their doll making. Sometimes, the dolls were used as toys for children. Other dolls were made to represent characters from Mi'kmaq stories. They were used to pass traditional stories down to younger generations.

Make a Porcupine-quill Bracelet

Materials

A mix of long, narrow beads and short, round beads
String, coloured wool, or leather
Scissors
A pencil

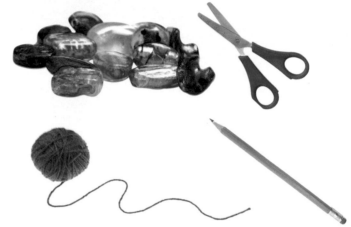

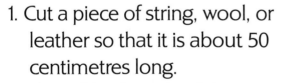

1. Cut a piece of string, wool, or leather so that it is about 50 centimetres long.
2. Thread both ends of the string through a single round bead. This will form a loop at one end.
3. Push a pencil through the loop to keep the string from being pulled all the way through the bead.

There should now be two strands of string falling from the bead. These two strands will form your bracelet.

4. Thread a long, narrow bead onto each strand.
5. Thread three round beads onto each strand. Continue this pattern until the bracelet is long enough to fit around your wrist.

6. Finish by threading both cords together through two round beads.
7. Take the pencil out of the loop.
8. Thread one cord through the loop.
9. Tie the two cords together with a double knot. Trim the ends with scissors.
10. Your bracelet is now complete. Slip it onto your wrist to wear.

Glossary

First Nation: a member of Canada's Aboriginal community who is not Inuit or Métis

migration: the movement from one place to another with the change of seasons

preserve: to keep food from rotting

spirituality: a person's faith

Index